T0381231

Freckles

DONNA TAGLIABRACCI

iUniverse books may be ordered through booksellers or by contacting:

iUniverse
1663 Liberty Drive
Bloomington, IN 47403
www.iuniverse.com
1-800-Authors (1-800-288-4677)

ISBN: 978-1-5320-7509-4 (sc)
ISBN: 978-1-5320-7510-0 (e)

Library of Congress Control Number: 2019908741

Print information available on the last page.

iUniverse rev. date: 07/11/2019

Freckles

In memory of Patricia Chapman McCracken who will be remembered as having a lively spirit and was unstoppable when she set her mind to something.

August 13, 1962 - March 20, 2018

Trish was nine in grade four. She was noticing other girls and boys her age and thought that they had some pretty cool qualities that she didn't have.

They had qualities or experiences that she thought were so great that she was going to get them no matter what she had to do. A girl at school who had recently broken her leg roller skating came to school with a large cast on her leg.

Trish who noticed everything, saw all of the attention the other girl was getting from all of her classmates. Girls and boys rushed to sign her cast in magic marker, ran to get her what she needed, and excitedly spoke to her as if she was a princess. While she was in the hospital, she received gifts and was waited on hand and foot.

Boy, thought Trish, it seems that the thing to do is to have a broken leg. Then I would get all that attention and gifts. So filled with determination she set out to break her leg.

She tried jumping off the tenth stair, fell off her bike on purpose, and jumped off the roof with a sheet as a parachute. But her leg did not break. All she did was get scrapes and bruises.

Then her brother got tonsillitis. He had to go to the hospital and after his operation he got ice cream, popsicles, jello, and lots of presents. It sure looked like the thing to get thought Trish. So she set out to get tonsillitis. She stole his popsicle, drank from his pop can, and tried to breathe his air when he was sleeping. But it didn't work. She didn't catch tonsillitis.

At school, she saw a really tall girl. Trish thought that this girl was beautiful with her long blonde hair and long slim legs. Boys stared at her when she walked by as if she was the only girl in the universe.

Apparently this was the thing to be. So Trish set out to be tall. She started by hanging by her arms on the ring bar at school for ten minutes at a time for seven days, but when she measured herself, she was still the same. She got no taller.

While sitting on the swing one day, Trish noticed a girl who had the most beautiful clear skin she had ever seen. Trish had freckles. Freckles were not the thing to have. So she set out to get rid of them. She bought three different types of cream, scrubbed her face with abrasive soap, and even made a witches potion with rose petals. Nothing worked. She was doomed to have freckles forever. Tired and frustrated, Trish gave up. She would never have those things which she thought were the things to have.

Trish became quiet and started to mope around. Then she noticed that her little brother was crying. He was crying because it hurt when he talked, it hurt when he swallowed, and he had trouble sleeping. Maybe tonsillitis wasn't the thing to have.

The girl who broke her leg wasn't getting much attention anymore. She missed out on the soccer tournament, couldn't dance at the sock hop, and took half and hour to get down the stairs with crutches. Maybe a broken leg wasn't the thing to have.

Then she saw the tall girl hit her head on a sign at the school and had a headache for an hour. Not many boys talked to her because they were all much shorter than she was in grade four. She was so tall that she towered over all the boys and no one would ask her to dance. Maybe being tall wasn't the thing to be.

Then Trish went to the last dance of the year. There was a really cute boy there that she had a crush on for the last year, but was too shy to talk to him. She thought to herself that he would probably like the beautiful girl with clear skin standing over by the D.J

Thinking for a long time about being tall, having tonsillitis, a broken leg and having no freckles, she was in her own little world. She didn't hear the boy come up to her and ask her to dance. He asked her again when he got her attention, and she couldn't believe it.

He liked her freckles and thought she was cute. Apparently the thing to be was just herself. Just Trish.